PUNS
for
Children

PUNS
for
Children

Winner of the
Pullet Surprise

by
Ninki Mallet

Also for children:
Please say Thank You
My Old Dog
Hakuna Matata – African
 Wisdom for Children
Bill & Coo

Cookbooks:
See Bangkok and Eat
See Thailand and Eat

About the author:

Ninki Mallet began her career in the film industry in Italy and then went on to being a columnist in South-East Asia writing books on cooking and living as an ex-patriot in a foreign land.

She has produced feature films, raised kids, had pets, and now writes for children and adults.

Introduction.

If you've ever heard a knock-knock joke, you've experienced the often groan-inducing form of humor known as a pun.

A pun is not always funny, but it is always a play on words. A pun can be made up in several different ways, based on the meaning or sonics of the words involved.

A pun is a word play wherein one word has two meanings. This gives a double meaning to the sentence, which is purposely done for a humorous effect.

Words could sound alike but have different meanings, like 'jeans' and 'genes', or they could be spelled the same but have two or more meanings, like the word 'club'

A knock-knock joke depends on the use of a pun: "Knock-Knock!" "Who's there?" "Orange." "Orange who?" "Orange you going to let me in?"

English is full of different figures of speech, which make it such a beautiful spoken language.

Learning figures of speech is a really hard task for children. It's difficult to remember what the figures of speech mean, how they are used, where they are used and on top of it all, their spellings.

One such figure of speech is a pun, and it can be taught with a great amount of fun, which is exactly what it is supposed to do.

There are not really one-word pun examples, because a pun almost always needs to be used in a setting so that it can create a word play.

Using different teaching methods can help children understand this part of grammar a lot better and forever.

Please enjoy.

What does Tarzan say about swinging through the Jungle?
"It's de-vine."

What do you call an insect that flies out of jail?
A free bee.

What do you call a rodent with rhythm?
A rat-a-tat-tat.

A man's home is his castle, *in a manor of speaking.*

How do you know when Santa is in the room?
You can feel his presents.

What do sheep sing to you on your birthday?
"Happy Birthday to Ewe!"

Knock-knock!
Who's there?
Aries.
Aries who?
Aries a reason I talk this way.

Knock-knock!
Who's there?
Ashby.
Ashby who?
Ashby in my fireplace.

Knock-knock!
Who's there?
Cash.
Cash who?
No thanks, but I'd like some
peanuts.

A gossip is someone with a great *sense of rumor.*

Where did people dance in Medieval times?
    In knight clubs.

What did one letter say to the other?
    "You send me."

Knock-knock!
  Who's there?
Bridle.
  Bridle who?
Bridle light of the silvery moon.

Knock-knock!
  Who's there?
Wilma.
  Wilma who?
Wilma ride be here soon?

Knock-knock!
  Who's there?
Doris.
  Doris who?
Doris locked, that's why I'm
knocking.

Knock-knock!
Who's there?
Banana.
Banana who?
Knock-knock!
Who's there?
Banana.
Knock-knock!
Who's there?
Banana.
Knock-knock!
Who's there?
Orange.
Orange who?
Orange you glad I didn't say
banana again?

BALLROOM:
   *A nursery for crying
babies.*

Knock-knock!
Who's there?
Oink oink.
Oink oink who?
Make up your mind; are you a
pig or an owl?

Knock-knock!
Who's there?
Me.
Me who?
No, seriously, it's just me.
I'm telling you a knock-knock
joke.

Knock-knock!
Who's there?
Honey bee.
Honeybee who?
Honey, be a dear and get me a
soda.

Knock-knock!
Who's there?
Cows go.
Cows go who?
No, cows go moo.

At a hearing aid center:
'Let us give you some sound advice'

Who do African antelopes listen to for the news?
Gnus.

Knock-knock!
Who's there?
Cook.
Cook who?
Cuckoo yourself; I didn't come
here to be insulted.

Knock-knock!
Who's there?
Lena.
Lena who?
Lena over here and give me a
big hug.

Knock-knock!
Who's there?
Madam.
Madam who?
Madam foot got caught in the
door.

I wanted to be a stenographer, but they told me *they are not short-handed at the moment.*

What do a mother deer, a baker, and a banker all have in common?
They all have a little doe.

Which planet is the dirtiest?
Pollute-o

DOCTOR: "Nurse, how is that little boy doing, the one who swallowed ten quarters?"
NURSE: *"No change yet"*.

Wouldn't it be funny if a film developer had a negative attitude?

SNOWMAN: "How are you doing?"
SNOWBALL: *"Snow-snow"*.

Without geometry, *life is pointless.*

What are the best desserts in the ocean?
Octo-pie.

What do monks eat for dinner?
Holy Chow!

Knock-knock!
Who's there?
Cheese.
Cheese who?
Cheese a jolly good fellow.

Knock-knock!
Who's there?
Ida.
Ida who?
Ida come over bud I godda code
in my doze.

Knock-knock!
Who's there?
Zeke.
Zeke who?
Zeke ze truth and it vil zet you
free.

What did the Easter Bunny say about its eggs?

"They're to die for."

What did the Mommy Lima Bean say to the Baby Lima Bean?

"Have you bean good"?

What did one potato say to the other potato?

"Keep your eyes peeled."

A man in Paris nearly got away with stealing several paintings from the Louvre.

But after planning the crime, breaking in, evading security, getting out and escaping with the goods, he was captured only 2 blocks away when his Econoline van ran out of gas.

When asked how he could have overlooked such an obvious error he replied:

"I had no Monet to buy Degas to make the Van Gogh."

I considered going into the ministry but I didn't have *an altar ego.*

What's the best way for a vegetable to send a message to another vegetable?
Pea-mail.

How do you fire people who repair watches?
Tell them their time is up.

Knock-knock!
Who's there?
Ammonia.
Ammonia who?
Ammonia poor little sparrow.

Knock-knock!
Who's there?
Seymour.
Seymour who?
Seymour birds with binoculars.

Knock-knock!
Who's there?
Telly.
Telly who?
Telly phone for you.

What is a theorist?

The part of the body that connects your hand to your arm.

What city is the joke capital of America?

Oma-ha.

What do you call a seamstress who is not very good?

Sew-so.

Knock-knock!
Who's there?
Cereal.
Cereal who?
Cereal pleasure to meet you.

Knock-knock!
Who's there?
Woody.
Woody who?
Woody mind if I come in?

Knock-knock!
Who's there?
Sara.
Sara who?
Sara way outta here – I'm
completely lost.

At a pizza shop:
*7 days without pizza
makes one weak*

What do a cat, a writer, and a kite have in common?
They all have tails.

How does a cowboy cross the ocean?
On his seahorse.

Knock-knock!
Who's there?
Cameron,
Cameron who?
Cameron film are needed to take
the pictures.

Knock-knock!
Who's there?
July.
July who?
July or tell the truth?

Knock-knock!
Who's there?
Abby.
Abbey who?
Abbey home for dinner.

On a Scientist's door:
Gone Fission

CATALYST:
What a cat takes along when shopping at the supermarket.

APPOINT:
That sharp thing at the end of your pencil.

Knock-knock!
Who's there?
Baby owl.
Baby owl who?
Baby owl see you later, maybe not!

Knock-knock!
Who's there?
Emil.
Emil who?
A meal sounds really good right now, I'm hungry.

Knock-knock!
Who's there?
Titus.
Titus who?
He Titus shoes much too tight.

A woman has twins, and gives them up for adoption.

One of them goes to a family in Egypt and is named Amal. The other goes to a family in Spain and they name him Juan.

Years later, Juan sends a picture of himself to his Mom. Upon receiving the picture, she tells her husband that she wishes she also had a picture of Amal.

Her husband responds:
"But they are twins. If you've seen Juan, you've seen Amal."

At the electric company:
We would be de-lighted if you send in your bill. However, if you don't, *you* will be.

What do you call a man who likes to cook?
Stew.

What is a seal's favorite card game?
Go fish.

Knock-knock!
Who's there?
Amelia.
Amelia who?
Amelia package last week, did you get it?

Knock-knock!
Who's there?
Ken.
Ken who?
Ken I please go out and play?

Knock-knock!
Who's there?
Kenya.
Kenya who?
Kenya not hear me knockin' on the door?

Did you hear about the Buddhist who refused his dentist's Novocain during root canal work?
He wanted to transcend dental medication.

How do you compliment the cook?
Tell her she's a dish.

DENTIST: "Asar, you're not brushing your teeth well enough. Do you know what comes after decay?"
ASAR: "De 'L'?"

Knock-knock!
Who's there?
Abyssinia.
Abyssinia who?
Abyssinia when I get back.

Knock-knock!
Who's there?
Yule.
Yule who?
Yule be sorry if you eat all that candy.

Knock-knock!
Who's there?
Janette.
Janette who?
Janette any fish today?

A NEUTRON walks into a bar:
  "I'd like a beer."
The BARTENDER promptly
serves up a beer.
NEUTRON: "How much will
that be?"
BARTENDER: "*For you? No
charge.*"

ANTELOPE:
  *When insects run away and get
  married.*

KIDNAP:
  When a baby goat takes sleeps.

Did you hear about the optometrist who fell into a lens grinder?
And made a spectacle of himself?

DEBATE:
What you put on your fishing hook.

Why did the man put bandages on his living room window?
He was told the window had pains.

Knock-knock!
Who's there?
Beets.
Beets who?
Beets me, and I just also forgot
the joke.

Knock-knock!
Who's there?
Roman.
Roman who?
Roman around the
neighborhood and I thought I'd
drop in.

Knock-knock!
Who's there?
Trixie.
Trixie who?
Trixie treat and Happy
Halloween!

Doctors tell us there are over seven million people who are overweight.

These, of course, are only round figures.

What kind of shoes do ghosts wear?

Boo-ts.

How did the Geometry teacher grade her students?

Fair and square.

Knock-knock!
Who's there?
Baron.
Baron who?
Baron mind who you're talking
to.

Knock-knock!
Who's there?
Gladys.
Gladys who?
Gladys Friday.

Knock-knock!
Who's there?
Hutch.
Hutch who?
BLESS YOU!

Old electricians never move away, they just *lose contact.*

What did one acrobat say to the other acrobat?
    "I'm head over heels in love with you."

Wouldn't it be funny if an acupuncturist felt *pointless?*

There was a man who entered a local pun contest.

He sent in ten different puns, in the hope that at least one pun would win. *Unfortunately, no pun in ten did.*

What do you call painting classes for sheriffs? *Marshall Arts.*

BEN: "Why did you jump in the pool?"
JERRY: "*I went off the deep end*".

There were two ships.

One had red paint, one had blue paint.

They collided.

At last report, the survivors were marooned.

What do maids like to do in their spare time?

Play mop-scotch.

MISS MARIA: "Where was the music teacher last week?"

PRINCIPAL: *"She had minor surgery."*

Knock-knock!
Who's there?
Adelia.
Adelia who?
Adelia the cards after you cut
the pack.

Knock-knock!
Who's there?
Mountain.
Mountain who?
Mountain a horse is hard.

Knock-knock!
Who's there?
Rhoda.
Rhoda who?
Rhoda scooter all across town to
get to your house.

I went to the butchers the other day and I bet him $50 that he couldn't reach the meat off the top shelf.

He said: *"No, the steaks are too high."*

What did the fish teacher say to her pupils?

"Stand up, gills and buoys".

JOE: "Do you know where to catch your flight when you get to the airport?"

MOE: *"Of course I do – it will be plane to see."*

Knock-knock!
  Who's there?
Avery.
  Avery who?
Avery time I come to your house
we have to go through this!

Knock-knock!
  Who's there?
Disguise.
  Disguise who?
Disguise the best comedian I
ever heard.

Knock-knock!
  Who's there?
Randy.
  Randy who?
Randy whole way and I'm all
outta breath.

I fired my masseuse today.
She just rubbed me the wrong way.

How did Ninki write this book?
She had the right stuff.

Why did the photographer like
to take friends with him when
he went on a job?
He liked to shoot the breeze.

MAN: "Doctor, I don't understand what is going on with me. It's really strange, sometimes I feel like a teepee."

The Doctor thinks about it for a while and then urges the man to continue.

MAN: "And sometimes I feel like a wigwam."

DOCTOR: *"Oh, I wouldn't worry about it, you're just two tents."*

PATRICK walked into a diner and sat down at the counter for a bite.

Just as he was about to dip his hand into the pretzel bowl, he heard a voice say: "Hey, nice shirt!"

Looking around, PATRICK couldn't figure out where the voice was coming from.

Then he heard it again: "Hey, nice tie!"

Quickly, PATRICK turned his head again, but still no one was there.

"Hey, nice haircut!" said the voice a third time.

Just then the WAITRESS arrived to take PATRICK'S order.

"Excuse me," said PATRICK to the WAITRESS, "but I keep hearing this strange voice."

"Oh, pay no attention to them," said the WAITRESS.

"That's just the pretzels. They're complimentary"

What is a Witch's best subject in
school?
   Spelling.

How do you clean a sheep?
   You give it a baa-th.

When are most twins born?
   On Twos-day.

Knock-knock!
Who's there?
Arizona.
Arizona who?
Arizona room for one of us in
this town.

Knock-knock!
Who's there?
Pasture.
Pasture who?
Pasture bedtime and you'd
better go to sleep now.

Knock-knock!
Who's there?
Dewey.
Dewey who?
Dewey have a holiday next
Monday?

JACK: "I have a new pet frog."
JILL: "You already toad me that."
JACK: "Well, I also have a new pet rabbit."
JILL: "I don't want to hare about it."

What Planet is the most musical?
Neptune.

What do ghosts wear at the beach?
They wear sun scream.

Knock-knock!
Who's there?
Athena.
Athena who?
Athena reindeer landing on your roof.

Knock-knock!
Who's there?
Eugene.
Eugene who?
Eugene's have a big rip in them.

Knock-knock!
Who's there?
Cassius.
Cassius who?
Cassius good to have in the bank.

Knock-knock!
Who's there?
Colin.
Colin who?
Colin all cars, colin all cars!

Knock-knock!
Who's there?
Carl.
Carl who?
Carl your Grandpa because he misses hearing from you.

Knock-knock!
Who's there?
Terra.
Terra who?
Terra piece of paper outta your notebook so you can write this down.

At the Amusement Park, L'IL ERIC stepped forward and plopped his money down at the ticket booth.

L'IL ERIC: "I want to go on the Mission to the Moon ride."

ATTENDANT: *"Sorry, the Moon is full right now."*

What is the best time to cook eggs?

On Fry-days.

ANTIFREEZE:

When your Dad's sister gets a bad cold.

Knock-knock!
Who's there?
Alexia.
Alexia who?
Alexia one more time to open
this door!

Knock-knock!
Who's there?
Duncan.
Duncan who?
Duncan chocolate chip cookies in
your milk is really yummy.

Knock-knock!
Who's there?
Skipper.
Skipper who?
Skipper class and your teacher
will be real mad.

SHERLOCK HOLMES:
"Watson, I believe the victim ate poisoned pistachios."
DR. WATSON: *"Sounds like a nut case to me, Holmes."*

TEACHER: "Use the word 'apparent' in a sentence."
ASHTON: *"When we come to Open House Night, we have to bring apparent."*

Why did the canary land on the boulder?
Because he was a rock singer.

Knock-knock!
Who's there?
Heaven.
Heaven who?
Heaven seen ya in such a long time!

Knock-knock!
Who's there?
Alba.
Alba who?
Alba in the kitchen if you need me.

Knock-knock!
Who's there?
Boris.
Boris who?
Boris with many more of those knock-knock jokes and we'll be leaving.

Knock-knock!
Who's there?
Cassie.
Cassie who?
Cassie the forest for the trees.

Knock-knock!
Who's there?
Lotta.
Lotta who?
Lotta help you are – I had to
wash the car all by myself.

Knock-knock!
Who's there?
Bennett.
Bennett who?
Bennett the fridge again for
leftovers?

I went to a seafood disco rave
last week *and pulled a mussel.*

What do cats send their
sweethearts on Valentine's Day?
Love litters.

Why did the ice sculptor win so
many awards?
His statues were cool.

Knock-knock!
Who's there?
Cumin.
Cumin who?
Cumin side, it's freezin' out
there!

Knock-knock!
Who's there?
Adore.
Adore who?
Adore is what I'm knocking on!

Knock-knock!
Who's there?
Annie.
Annie who?
Annie thing you can do I can do
better!

I was on an elevator the other day, and the operator kept calling me "son".

I said: "Why do you keep calling me son? You're not my father."

He said: "I brought you up, didn't I?"

What do birds do for entertainment?

They tell yolks.

Why are sheep bad dog trainers?

Because ewe can't teach an old dog new tricks.

Which president was least
guilty?
　　Abraham Lincoln.
　　Why?
　　Because he is in a cent.

It's funny when an auto
mechanic *is exhausted.*

What has letters and dashes?
　　*The mailman who is
running a little late.*

Knock-knock!
Who's there?
Auntie.
Auntie who?
Auntie glad to see me again?

Knock-knock!
Who's there?
Celeste.
Celeste who?
Celeste time I'm going to lend
you any money!

Knock-knock!
Who's there?
Clare.
Clare who?
Clare your throat before you
speak, please

Diet slogan:
   Are you going the wrong weigh?

Hardworking Farmer's Motto:
   No pain no grain

CHIP: "I broke all my teeth in carpentry school."
CHAP: "How did you manage to do that?"
CHIP: "I was *chewing my nails.*"

A young boy had a job bagging groceries at a supermarket.

One day the store decided to install a machine for squeezing fresh orange juice.

The young boy liked the machine, and he asked if he could be allowed to work the machine.

The store manager refused, but the young boy couldn't understand why.

The store manager explained it to him, *"Sorry, kid, but baggers can't be juicers."*

What did the black belt karate expert say to her husband?

"Only thirty chopping days to Christmas."

FIRST MATCHBOX: "What's new?"

SECOND MATCHBOX: *"Flame old thing."*

When Volkswagens retire, do they go to the *Old Volks' Home?*

Why was the policeman fired from his part-time job at the bowling alley?

He kept giving tickets for changing lanes.

Mary Poppins decided to move
to Southern California where
she began telling people's
fortunes.

She didn't read their palms
or tealeaves; she just smelled
people's breath.

The sign in the room where
she told their fortunes read:

'SUPER CALIFORNIA MYSTIC
EXPERT HALITOSIS'

Her 7-year-old grandson
surprised a grandmother one
morning when he made her
coffee.

She drank what was the
worst cup of coffee in her life.
When she got to the bottom
there were three of those little
green army men in the cup.

She said, "Honey, what are
the army men doing in my
coffee?"

Her grandson said:

*"Grandma, it says on TV
the best part of waking up is
soldiers in your cup!"*

Two boll weavels grew up in South Carolina.

One went to Hollywood and became a famous actor.

The other stayed behind in the cotton fields and never amounted to much.

The second one, naturally, became known as *the lesser of two weevils.*

What did the coach say to his losing team of snakes?
You can't venom all.

The dumbest cowboy in the world went to an insurance office to get a policy.
INSURANCE AGENT: "Did you ever have any accidents?"
COWBOY: "No, sir! But one time a horse kicked me in the head and a rattlesnake bit me on the toe."
INSURANCE AGENT: "Don't you call those accidents?"
COWBOY: *"Why, heck no, mister! They did it on purpose!"*

How's business at the perfume factory?

Not good. Business is bad. *We lost every scent.*

I don't believe in séances, but I went to one just to see what it was like.

The psychic was doing his thing and grinning from ear to ear.

I guessed his merriment was due to the fact that he was fooling a gullible public and I gave him a poke in the nose. You can guess the rest.

I was arrested for striking a happy medium.

My friend loves to make pottery, but to me it's just *kiln time.*

What do computers and great tennis teams have in common? *Both have really good servers.*

Where do pigs go on vacation? *To the Sows Pacific.*

As migration approached, two elderly vultures doubted they could make the trip south, so they decided to go by plane.

When they checked their baggage, the attendant noticed that they were carrying two dead raccoons.

"Do you wish to check the raccoons through as luggage?" she asked.

"No, thanks," replied the vultures. *"They're carrion."*

A chicken crossing the road is *poultry in motion.*

A three-legged dog walks into a saloon in the Old West.

He sidles up to the bar and announces: *"I'm lookin' for the man who shot my Paw."*

What do you call a shark with glass slippers?

Fin-derella.

This Kentucky horse breeder had a filly that won every race in which she was entered.

But as she got older she became very temperamental.

He soon found that when he raced her in the evening, she would win handily, but when she raced during the day she would come in dead last.

He consulted the top veterinarians and horse psychologists to no avail. He finally had to give up because the horse had become a real *nightmare.*

Reading whilst sunbathing
makes you *well red.*

What did the spider say to the
fly?
   *"Would you like to come to
the webbing"?*

Why do nine out of ten roosters
have little duck decals on their
alarm clocks?
   *So they can get up for work
at the quack of dawn.*

An elephant was drinking out of a river one day, when he spotted a turtle asleep on a log.

He ambled on over and kicked it clear across the river.

"What did you do that for?" asked a passing giraffe.

"Because I recognized it as the same turtle that took a nip out of my trunk 53 years ago."

"Wow, what a memory," commented the giraffe.

"Yes," said the elephant, *"turtle recall."*

This duck walks into a bar and orders a beer.

"Four bucks," says the bartender.

"Put it on my bill." says the duck.

When two egotists meet, *it's an I for an I.*

What stone-carved National Mountain Monument honors presidential dogs?

Mutt Rushmore.

JACK: "Hey, Don! How's your new pet fish doing? You told me he was really something special.

DON: "To tell you the truth, I'm really disappointed in him. The guy who sold him to me said I could teach him to sing like a bird."

JACK: "You bought a fish because you thought you could teach him to sing like a bird? I can't believe it!"

DON: "Well, yeah. After all, he's a parrot fish."

JACK: "I hate to tell you this, but while you might be able to teach a parrot bird to sing, you're never going to get anywhere with a parrot fish."

DON: "That's what you think! He can sing all right. The thing is, he keeps singing off-key. It's driving me crazy. *Do you know how hard it is to tuna fish?*"

What did the chimpanzee say when his sister had a baby?
Well, I'll be a monkey's uncle.

What kind of car does Mickey Mouse drive?
A mini van.

Who invented fractions?
King Henry the 1/8.

Knock-knock!
 Who's there?
Artichoke.
 Artichoke who?
Artie choke when he swallowed
his Yo-Yo!

Knock-knock!
 Who's there?
Manuel.
 Manuel who?
Manuel be sorry if you don't get
a move on.

Knock-knock!
 Who's there?
Fido.
 Fido who?
If Fidon't come back, send out a
search party.

What did the toy store sign say?
'Don't feed the animals. They
are already stuffed'

I phoned the zoo, *but the lion
was busy.*

Two attractive female birds
were showing off in front of
some males.
Both had spent two hours
at the hairdresser, but it was
the *curly bird that got the perm.*

Knock-knock!
Who's there?
Annetta.
Annetta who?
Annetta joke like that and I'm
outta here!

Knock-knock!
Who's there?
Abie.
Abie who?
Abie C D E F G H ...

Knock-knock!
Who's there?
Possum
Possum who?
Possum ketchup on my
hamburger, please.

One horse said to another, "Your pace is familiar *but I don't remember the mane.*"

Don't believe what you hear about fleas and ticks.
It's all lice.

What do you call a baby monkey?
A chimp off the old block.

It's okay to watch an elephant take a bath *because they always have their trunks on.*

What musical is about a train conductor?
My Fare, Lady.

Did you hear about the crab in financial difficulty?
It was starting *to feel the pinch.*

What did the farmer say to the
cow that had no milk?
   "You are an udder failure!"

An invisible man married an
invisible woman.
   *The kids were nothing to
look at.*

Show me a piano falling down a
mineshaft, and I'll show you
A-flat minor.

I've been to the dentist many times so *I know the drill.*

Why are fish so smart?
   Because they live in schools.

How does a witch doctor ask a girl to dance?
   "Voodoo like to dance with me?"

Two antennas met on a roof, fell in love and got married.
The ceremony wasn't much, *but the reception was brilliant*

Where do polar bears vote?
The North Poll.

When a clock is hungry *it goes back four seconds.*

Time flies like an arrow.
Fruit flies like a banana.

What animals do you find on
legal documents?
Seals.

Every calendar's days
are numbered.

A bicycle cannot stand on its own *because it's two tired.*

The man who fell into an upholstery machine *is fully re-covered.*

What's purple and five thousand miles long?
  The Grape Wall of China.

What did the Judge say when
the skunk walked into the
courtroom?

    "Odor in the court!"

Two fish are in a tank.
One says to the other, *"Err ...
how do you drive this thing?"*

What Old West Sheriff never
said much?

    Quiet Earp.

What do you call a sleeping
bull?
    A bulldozer.

Yesterday is history, tomorrow
is a mystery, but today is a gift.
    *That's why it's called the
present.*

In a Democracy your vote
counts.
    In Feudalism, your Count
votes.

How do celebrities stay cool?
They have lots of fans.

You feel stuck with your *debt if you can't budge it.*

If you want to make money as a comedian you've got to have *the cents of humor.*

A horse walks into a bar.
The bartender says,
"So, why the long face?"

The roundest knight at King
Arthur's table was Sir
Cumference.
He acquired his size *from
too much pi.*

Maid Marian wrote a letter to
her parents when she was at
summer camp.
Dear Mom and Dad, the
days are okay, but I'm having
trouble with the knights.

A man goes into a restaurant for a Christmas breakfast while in his hometown for the holidays. After looking over the menu he says, "I'll just have the Eggs Benedict."

His order comes a while later and it's served on a huge fancy chrome plate.

He asks the waiter, "What's with the fancy plate?"

The waiter replies, *"There's no plate like chrome for the hollandaise."*

What do you get from a
pampered cow?
You get spoiled milk.

How does the farmer fit more
pigs on his farm?
He builds a styscraper.

Why isn't gambling allowed in
Africa?
Because of all the cheetahs.

If you don't pay your exorcist,
will you get repossessed?

Why can't you keep a secret in a
bank?
   Because of all the tellers.

What do you get when you cross
James Bond with a bagpipe?
   A spy with a license to kilt.

This little snail bought a little car and took it to the body shop to have it painted.

The service man asked him exactly what he wanted done, and the little snail said he wanted little S's painted all around and all over his car.

The service man asked him why, and the little snail answered, "When people see me in my car, I want them to say, *"Look at that S-car-go!"*

What do you call a cow that
won't give milk?
   It's a milk dud.

What extras do werewolves
order for their cars?
   A full-moon roof.

MAX: "I lost my fish.   What
should I do?"
DAX: *"Have you checked the lost
and flounder department?"*

The Skunk family had two little skunks they called In and Out.

One day little In disappeared.

Mother Skunk, Father Skunk and young Out spent hours looking for him, getting more worried all the time.

In the end the parents went home to have a cup of tea, but Out said he'd continue searching for a while.

Half an hour later he returned home, with a tired In following behind him.

"However did you find him?" asked Father Skunk.

"In-stinct," replied Out.

Why do you think the lion spit
out the clown?
    He spat him out *because he
tasted funny.*

When does a well-dressed lion
look like a weed?
    When he's a dandelion.

What do you get when a chicken
lays an egg on a sloping roof?
    An egg roll.

"Doctor, Doctor, I feel like biscuits!"

"What, you mean those square ones?"

"Yes!"

"The ones you put butter on?"

"Yes!"

"Oh, you're crackers."

Knock-knock!
Who's there?
Burton.
Burton who?
Burton the hand is worth two in
the bush.

Knock-knock!
Who's there?
Canoe.
Canoe who?
Canoe help me get to the next
game level?

Knock-knock!
Who's there?
Musket.
Musket who?
Musket my jacket, it's freezing
outside.

Why is a fish so easy to weigh?
Because it has its own scales.

Sign at a car dealership:
'The best way to get back on your feet - miss a car payment.'

PATIENT: "Doctor, Doctor, I think I'm a battery."
DOCTOR: "How do you feel about that?"
PATIENT: *"Well, it has its pluses and minuses".*

Knock-knock!
Who's there?
Miniature.
Miniature who?
Miniature open the door, I'll tell ya!

Knock-knock!
Who's there?
Nemo
Nemo who?
Nemo time to get ready.

Knock-knock!
Who's there?
Formosa.
Formosa who?
Formosa the day I just watch TV.

What do you get when you cross
a snake and a pie?
A pie-thon.

What did the security guard at
the greenhouse say when he
heard a noise?
"Who grows there?"

PATIENT: "Doctor, I feel like a
pair of curtains."
DOCTOR: *"Well, pull yourself
together then."*

Knock-knock!
Who's there?
Mitzi.
Mitzi who?
Mitzi door shut, you'll never know!

Knock-knock!
Who's there?
Morris.
Morris who?
Morris another day.

Knock-knock!
Who's there?
Saint Bernard.
Saint Bernard who?
Saint Bernard to the pet store to buy some dog food.

What fish only swims at night?
A starfish.

Why did the bus stop?
Because it saw the zebra crossing.

I used to look for gold, *but it didn't pan out.*

How do eels get around the seabed?

They go by octobus.

I used to be a banker, *but lost interest in the work.*

WANTED:

'Domestic cat wanted to do light mousework.'

The big chess tournament was taking place at the Plaza Hotel in New York.

After the first day's competition, many of the winners were sitting around in the foyer talking about their matches and bragging about their wonderful play.

After a few drinks they started getting louder and louder until finally, the desk clerk couldn't take it any more and kicked them out.

The next morning the Manager called the clerk into his office and told him there had been many complaints about his being so rude to the hotel guests. Instead of kicking them out, he should have just asked them to be less noisy.

The clerk responded, "I'm sorry, but if there's one thing I can't stand, *it's chess nuts boasting in an open foyer.*"

I used to be a baker, *but I didn't make enough dough.*

ART TEACHER: "The picture of the horse is good, but where is the wagon?"
PUPIL: *"The horse will draw it."*

I used to be a blackjack host, but was offered *a better deal.*

What do bees do with their honey?
They cell it.

I used to work for Budweiser, but then *I got canned.*

What did Juliecat say when she stepped out on the balcony?
"Ro-meow, Ro-meow..."

Snow White received a camera as a gift.

She happily took pictures of the Dwarfs and their surroundings.

When she finished her first batch she took the film to be developed.

After a week or so she went to pick up the finished photos.

The clerk said the photos were not back from the processor.

Needless to say, she was disappointed and began to cry.

The clerk, trying to console her, said,

"Don't worry. Someday your prints will come."

I used to be a butler, but found the work *wasn't my cup of tea.*

Two Eskimos sitting in a kayak were chilly, but when they lit a fire in the craft it sank – proving once and for all *that you can't have your kayak and heat it, too.*

I used to be a carpenter, but then *I got bored.*

Two atoms are walking down the street and they run in to each other.

One says to the other, "Are you all right?"

"No, I lost an electron!"

"Are you sure?"

"Yeah, I'm positive."

I used to be a doctor, *but then I lost patients.*

What should you give an injured baby alligator?

Gator-aid.

A hungry lion was roaming through the jungle looked for something to eat.

He came across two men.

One was sitting under a tree reading a book; the other was typing away on his typewriter.

The lion quickly pounced on the man reading the book and devoured him.

Even the king of the jungle knows that readers digest and writers cramp.

I used to be a hotel clerk, *but then I had reservations.*

At the supermarket I saw a man and a woman wrapped in a barcode.

I asked: *"Are you two an item?"*

I used to be a marathon runner, *but couldn't stand the agony of de feet.*

Knock-knock!
Who's there?
Barbra.
Barbra who?
Barbra black sheep, have you
any wool...

Knock-knock!
Who's there?
Tijuana.
Tijuana who?
Tijuana see my cat's kittens?

Knock-knock!
Who's there?
Feline.
Feline who?
I'm feline fine. How about you?

I used to be a railroad
conductor, but my boss found
out *I wasn't trained.*

MR. CAT: "They're building a
kennel up the street."
MRS. CAT: "We've got to move
out of this neighborhood *before it
goes to the dogs.*"

What do you get when you cross
a pet spider with a pet hare?
A pet webbit.

Knock-knock!
Who's there?
Button.
Button who?
Button in is not polite.

Knock-knock!
Who's there?
Police.
Police who?
Police say Thank You – That's
one of the little books that Ninki
Mallet wrote.

Knock-knock!
Who's there?
Eddie.
Eddie who?
Eddie body home?

I used to be a road digger, *but I got re-trenched.*

I used to be a sanitation engineer, *but the city dumped me.*

I used to sell computer parts, *but then I lost my drive.*

Knock-knock!
Who's there?
Denise.
Denise who?
Denise are above your ankles.

Knock-knock!
Who's there?
Jaws.
Jaws who?
Jaws truly.

Knock-knock!
Who's there?
Avenue.
Avenue who?
Avenue heard the good news?

I used to be a taxi driver,
but I couldn't hack it.

I used to be a teacher, *but found
I didn't have enough class.*

I used to be a tennis instructor,
but it just wasn't my racket.

Once upon a time there were 2 canaries in a cage.

The male canary said to the female, "Can I move over to your side of the cage?"

The female canary replied, "No, thanks!"

So he went back to his side of the cage but the next day he moved over to her side of the cage and asked, "I'm sorry I was so forward. Why don't we get to know each other first?"

To which she replied again, "No, thanks."

Resigning himself to return to his side of the cage, he asked, "Well, could we at least talk?"

This time she replied, "I'm so sorry I've been mean. *But I'm sick, and it's untweetable.*"

You'd never believe it, but I bumped into a famous stuntman in a motorcycle shop the other day.

He was complaining because he couldn't decide whether to buy a bike with a high top speed but poor acceleration, or one with lots of torque and a fast acceleration but a poor top speed.

Eventually he decided on the second one because it cost a lot less.

After all...torque is cheap.

I used to be a train driver
but I got sidetracked.

I used to be a transplant
surgeon, *but my heart just
wasn't in it.*

What overnight shipping
company do vampires use?
Necks Day Delivery.

Knock-knock!
Who's there?
France.
France who?
France of the family.

Knock-knock!
Who's there?
Bird A.
Bird A who?
Bird A parties are lotsa fun.

Knock-knock!
Who's there?
Icy.
Icy who?
Icy your dog had puppies again.

Two young boys were out in the woods on a camping trip, when they came upon this great brook. They stayed there all day, enjoying the fishing, which was big fun.

At the end of the day they vowed that they would meet, in 20 years, at the same place.

20 years later, they met and hiked to the spot near where they had been years before. They walked into the woods and before long came upon a brook.

One of the men said to the other, "This is the place."

The other replied, "No, it's not."

The first man said, "Yes, I recognize the clover growing on the bank on the other side."

To which the other man said, "Silly, *you can't tell a brook by its clover.*"

A baby pigeon was flying in the sky with his Mom.

He got very tired and said, "I can't make it, and I'm getting too tired,"

His Mom said, "Don't worry, I'll tie a piece of string to one of your legs and the other end to mine."

The baby pigeon started to cry.

"What's wrong?" said his Mom

The baby pigeon replied, *"I don't want to be pigeon towed."*

A film director is screen-testing Sylvester Stallone and Arnold Schwarzenegger for a new film about classical music composers.

Not having figured out whom to give which part to, he asks Sly who he would like to be.

Stallone says, "I like Mozart. I want to be Mozart."

So the director says, "Okay, you can be Mozart."

Then he turns to Arnie and says, "Whom would you like to play?"

And Arnie says, *"I'll be Bach."*

I used to be a Velcro salesman,
but couldn't stick with it.

OSCAR: "Did you ever see
'Cats' on Broadway?"
EMMY: "No, but once I saw
mice scamper down Fifth
Avenue."

WANT AD:
Vets needed to examine
Dalmatians –
Spot checkers.

Knock-knock!
  Who's there?
Omelet.
  Omlet who?
Omletting your dog out, is that okay?

Knock-knock!
  Who's there?
Pekingese.
  Pekingese who?
Pekingese boxes and you'll know what you're getting for Xmas.

Knock-knock.
  Who's there?
Hacienda.
  Hacienda who?
Hacienda the story!

The End.

Oranged you pleased it's all over?

79591784R00079

Made in the USA
Lexington, KY
24 January 2018